"But I Wouldn't Want to Live There!"

Wicked Wisdom from Seasoned Travelers

EDITED BY

**MICHAEL CADER AND
LISA CADER**

Running Press
Philadelphia, Pennsylvania

Excerpts from *The Lost Continent* by Bill Bryson copyright © 1990 by Bill Bryson,
reprinted by permission of HarperCollins Publishers. Excerpts from *You Gotta Play
Hurt* by Dan Jenkins copyright © 1991 by D & J Ventures, Inc., reprinted by
permission of Simon & Schuster, Inc. Excerpt from *Molly Ivins Can't Say That Can
She?* by Molly Ivins copyright © 1991 by Molly Ivins, reprinted by permission of
Random House, Inc.

Canadian representatives: General Publishing Co., Ltd., 30 Lesmill Road, Don Mills,
Ontario M3B 2T6. International representatives: Worldwide Media Services, Inc., 30
Montgomery Street, Jersey City, New Jersey 07302.

9 8 7 6 5 4 3 2 1
Digit on the right indicates the number of this printing.

Library of Congress Cataloging-in-Publication Number 93–83913

ISBN 1–56138–280–9

Cover design by Toby Schmidt
Cover illustration provided by Xonex International, Inc.
Interior design by Jacqueline Spadaro
Interior illustrations by Sarah McMenemy
Edited by Melissa Stein
Typography: CG Bodoni and Bodega Sans Light by Richard Conklin
Printed in the United States

This book may be ordered by mail from the publisher.
Please add $2.50 for postage and handling. *But try your bookstore first!*

Running Press Book Publishers
125 South Twenty-second Street
Philadelphia, Pennsylvania 19103

Contents

Introduction

"It's a nice place to visit, but I wouldn't want to live there!"

—ANONYMOUS

Have you noticed that no matter where you go in this world, no one likes people from any village, city, county, state, or country other than the one in which they live? Some people who reside less than an hour from major cities such as London or New York have never visited, because they are convinced that they will hate it.

Those of us who do travel return bearing stories of strange food, inexplicable languages, laughable currency, and mishaps along the way. Often, the best part of traveling is coming home and telling everyone what went wrong!

One person's Paris is another person's Baltimore or Detroit—it all depends upon which one you are visiting and where you live. *"But I Wouldn't Want to Live There!"* is a good-natured (though crankily-worded) accounting of everything "out there" that just doesn't measure up to wherever you happen to call home.

Getting There

Traveling is a fool's paradise.

RALPH WALDO EMERSON

Is there anything as horrible as starting on a trip? Once you're off, that's all right, but the last moments are earthquake and convulsion, and the feeling that you are a snail being pulled off your rock.

ANNE MORROW LINDBERGH

People travel for the same reason as they collect works of art: because the best people do it.

ALDOUS HUXLEY

Thanks to the Interstate Highway System, it is now possible to travel from coast to coast without seeing anything.

CHARLES KURALT

Getting There

To give you an idea of how fast we traveled: we left Spokane with two rabbits and when we got to Topeka, we still had only two.

BOB HOPE

Men travel faster now, but I do not know if they go to better things.

WILLA CATHER

A hundred years ago, it could take you the better part of a year to get from New York to California; whereas today, because of equipment problems at O'Hare, you can't get there at all.

DAVE BARRY

There are two kinds of travel in the United States, first class and third world.

BOBBY SLAYTON

In America there are two classes of travel—first class and with children.

ROBERT BENCHLEY

I've traveled more this year than any other living human being, and if I'd traveled any more I wouldn't be living.

WALTER F. MONDALE

I have found out that there ain't no surer way to find out whether you like people or hate them, than to travel with them.

MARK TWAIN

On a long journey even a straw weighs heavy.

SPANISH PROVERB

It is imperative when flying coach that you restrain any tendency toward the vividly imaginative. For although it may momentarily appear to be the case, it is not at all likely that the cabin is entirely inhabited by crying babies smoking inexpensive domestic cigars.

FRAN LEBOWITZ

Getting There

Never play peek-a-boo with a child on a long plane trip. There's no end to the game. Finally I grabbed him by the bib and said, "Look, it's always gonna be me!"

RITA RUDNER

The Baggage Carousel, where passengers traditionally gather at the end of a flight to spend several relaxing hours watching the arrival of luggage from some other flight . . .

DAVE BARRY

Except for Rothschilds and madmen, all first-class passengers travel on expense accounts.

RUSSELL BAKER

If God had intended us to fly, he would never have given us railways.

ATTRIBUTED TO MICHAEL FLANDERS

9

I like terra firma—the more firma, the less terra.

GEORGE S. KAUFMAN

Lovers of air travel find it exhilarating to hang poised between the illusion of immortality and the fact of death.

ALEXANDER CHASE

. . . airline insurance replaces the fear of death with the comforting prospect of cash.

CECIL BEATON

Companions: if you're travelling alone, beware of seatmates who by way of starting a conversation make remarks like, 'I just have to talk to someone—my teeth are spying on me' or 'Did you know that squirrels are the devil's oven mitts?'

MISS PIGGY

10

Getting There

. . . a luxury liner is really just a bad play surrounded by water.

CLIVE JAMES

Unhelpful Advice for Foreign Tourists: When travelling by train, remember that it is considered impolite not to help anyone who is doing the *Times* crossword puzzle.

PETER ALEXANDER

A railroad station? That was sort of a primitive airport, only you didn't have to take a cab 20 miles out of town to reach it.

RUSSELL BAKER

Nothing was more up to date when it was built, or more obsolete today, than the railroad station.

ADA LOUISE HUXTABLE

The most common of all antagonisms arises from a man's taking a seat beside you on the train, a seat to which he is completely entitled.

ROBERT BENCHLEY

It is easier to find a travelling companion than to get rid of one.

PEG BRACKEN

Fish & Visitors stink in three days.

BENJAMIN FRANKLIN

There is an infallible test for detecting a tourist in any metropolis in the world—simply look for a man standing in front of a cutlery or luggage shop with his mouth ajar, gazing vacantly in at the manicure sets, razor strops, and collar-boxes and jingling the change in his pockets.

S. J. PERELMAN

I have just arrived back home from Europe with 850,000 other half-wits who think that a summer not spent among the decay and mortification of the Old World is a summer squandered.

WILL ROGERS

Getting There

The major advantage of domestic travel is that, with a few exceptions such as Miami, most domestic locations are conveniently situated right here in the United States.

DAVE BARRY

. . . I was at a place called the Fractured Arms. . . . You can imagine how big my room was—when I closed the door, the doorknob got in bed with me. It was so small, even the mice were hunchback. I had a headache, the guy next door had to take the aspirin.

HENNY YOUNGMAN

Generally speaking, the length and grandness of a hotel's name are an exact opposite reflection of its quality. Thus the Hotel Central will prove to be a clean, pleasant place in a good part of town, and the Hotel Royal Majestic-Fantastic will be a fleabag next to a topless bowling alley.

MISS PIGGY

The great advantage of a hotel is that it's a refuge from your home life.

GEORGE BERNARD SHAW

He who travels to be amused, or to get somewhat which he does not carry, travels away from himself, and grows old even in youth among old things.

RALPH WALDO EMERSON

The truth is if you do them right, they're hard work. They're like an Outward Bound experience with diarrhea. We pay a lot of money to sleep in airports, lug around suitcases twice our body weight, eat food we can't identify, and put our lives in the hands of people we have never met before.

ERMA BOMBECK

When one realizes that his life is worthless he either commits suicide or travels.

EDWARD DAHLBERG

There is nothing more miserable in this world than to arrive in paradise looking like your passport picture.

ERMA BOMBECK

Travel is glamorous only in retrospect.

PAUL THEROUX

The American Frontier

It was wonderful to find America, but it would have been more wonderful to miss it.

MARK TWAIN

What a pity, when Christopher Columbus discovered America, that he ever mentioned it.

MARGOT ASQUITH

The United States is the greatest single achievement of European civilization.

ROBERT BALMAIN MOWAT

America is a large, friendly dog in a small room. Every time it wags its tail it knocks over a chair.

ARNOLD TOYNBEE

15

America is the greatest of opportunities and the worst of influences.

GEORGE SANTAYANA

"Antiques" in America are touching. Everything over twenty-five years old seems to count as one.

T. H. WHITE

The American language is in a state of flux based on the survival of the unfittest.

CYRIL CONNOLLY

In the United States there is more space where nobody is than where anybody is. That's what makes America what it is.

GERTRUDE STEIN

Our country is too big for union, too sordid for patriotism, too democratic for liberty.

FISHER AMES

An asylum for the sane would be empty in America.

GEORGE BERNARD SHAW

To be a celebrity in America is to be forgiven everything.

MARY MCGRORY

America, where overnight success is both a legend and a major industry.

JOHN LEGGETT

Whoever wants to know the hearts and minds of America had better learn baseball.

JACQUES BARZUN

If you're going to America, bring your own food.

FRAN LEBOWITZ

17

"BUT I WOULDN'T WANT TO LIVE THERE!"

In America sex is an obsession, in other parts of the world it is a fact.

MARLENE DIETRICH

There's so much plastic in this culture that vinyl leopard skin is becoming an endangered synthetic.

LILY TOMLIN

What the United States does best is to understand itself. What it does worst is understand others.

CARLOS FUENTES

Every time Europe looks across the Atlantic to see the American eagle, it observes only the rear end of an ostrich.

H. G. WELLS

Good Americans, when they die, go to Paris.

THOMAS GOLD APPLETON

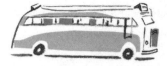

When good Americans die they go to
Paris; when bad Americans die they go
to America.

OSCAR WILDE

America—a country that has leapt from barbarism to decadence without touching civilization.

JOHN O'HARA

America is the only nation in history which miraculously has gone directly from
barbarism to degeneration without the usual interval of civilization.

GEORGE CLEMENCEAU

The only country in the world where failing to promote yourself is regarded as
being arrogant.

GARRY TRUDEAU

As for America, it is the ideal fruit of all your youthful hopes and reforms.
Everybody is fairly decent, respectable, domestic, bourgeois, middle-class, and
tiresome. There is absolutely nothing to revile except that it's a bore.

HENRY ADAMS

19

America, we found, occupied the curious dual role of skinflint and sucker, the usurer bent on exacting his pound of flesh and the hapless pigeon whose poke was a challenge to any smart grifter.

S. J. PERELMAN

The United States is the greatest law factory the world has ever known.

CHARLES EVANS HUGHES

America is the noisiest country that ever existed.

OSCAR WILDE

Our national flower is the concrete cloverleaf.

LEWIS MUMFORD

In all the countries of Europe, even Spain, the villages along the way are charming, but in the United States they are almost uniformly appalling.

H. L. MENCKEN

The American Frontier

The reason American cities are prosperous is that there is no place to sit down.

ALFRED J. TALLEY

The way to see America is from a lower berth about two in the morning, You've just left a station—it was the jerk pulling out that woke you—and you raise the curtain a bit between thumb and forefinger to look out.

JACQUES BARZUN

No one should be required to see America for the first time.

ANONYMOUS

America is a mistake, a giant mistake!

SIGMUND FREUD

The City

Cities are too big and too rich for beauty; they have outgrown themselves too many times.

NOEL PERRIN

The big cities of America are becoming Third World countries.

NORA EPHRON

I doubt if there is anything in the world uglier than a midwestern city.

FRANK LLOYD WRIGHT

American cities are like badger holes, ringed with trash—all of them—surrounded by piles of wrecked and rusting automobiles, and almost smothered with rubbish.

JOHN STEINBECK

The city is not a concrete jungle. It is a human zoo.

DESMOND MORRIS

Cities, like cats, will reveal themselves at night.

RUPERT BROOKE

In a real estate man's eye, the most exclusive part of the city is wherever he has a house to sell.

WILL ROGERS

To think that I should live cooped up in a great city, just to be pestered and plagued by people!

HENRIK IBSEN

The mobs of great cities add just so much to the support of pure government as sores do to the strength of the human body.

THOMAS JEFFERSON

"BUT I WOULDN'T WANT TO LIVE THERE!"

City life: Millions of people being lone-
some together.

HENRY DAVID THOREAU

It is a colossal opportunity to escape from life that brings yokels to the cities,
not just lust for money.

H. L. MENCKEN

As a remedy to life in society, I would suggest the big city. Nowadays, it is the
only desert within our means.

ALBERT CAMUS

If you would be known, and not know, vegetate in a village; if you would know,
and not be known, live in a city.

C. C. COLTON

The Country

There is nothing good to be had in the country, or, if there be, they will not let you have it.

WILLIAM HAZLITT

The country has charms only for those not obliged to stay there.

EDOUARD MANET

Anybody can be good in the country. There are no temptations there.

OSCAR WILDE

Country life is very good; in fact, the best—for cattle.

SYDNEY SMITH

A farm is an irregular patch of nettles, bounded by short-term notes, containing a fool and his wife who didn't know enough to stay in the city.

S. J. PERELMAN

"BUT I WOULDN'T WANT TO LIVE THERE!"

I see a little time in the country makes a man turn wild and unsociable, and only fit to converse with his horses, dogs, and his herds.

WILLIAM WYCHERLEY

I have never understood why anybody agreed to go on being rustic after about 1400.

KINGSLEY AMIS

To put it rather bluntly, I am not the type who wants to go back to the land; I am the type who wants to go back to the hotel.

FRAN LEBOWITZ

Suburbia is where the developer bulldozes out the trees, then names the streets after them.

BILL VAUGHN

I hate small towns because once you've seen the cannon in the park there's nothing else to do.

LENNY BRUCE

North, South, East, and West

The most serious charge that can be brought against New England is not Puritanism but February.

JOSEPH WOOD KRUTCH

Of course what the man from Mars will find out first about New England is that it is neither new nor very much like England.

JOHN GUNTHER

The swaggering underemphasis of New England.

HEYWOOD BROUN

Oliver Wendell Holmes says that Yankee Schoolmarms, the cider, and the salt codfish of the Eastern states are responsible for what he calls a nasal accent.

RUDYARD KIPLING

"BUT I WOULDN'T WANT TO LIVE THERE!"

Yankee, n. In Europe, an American. In the Northern States of our Union, a New Englander. In the Southern States the word is unknown. (See Damyank.)

AMBROSE BIERCE

Southerners are probably not more hospitable than New Englanders are; they are simply more willing to remind you of the fact that they are being hospitable.

RAY L. BIRDWHISTELL

Southerners can never resist a losing cause.

MARGARET MITCHELL

You may be Southern—but you're no Comfort.

DICK GREGORY

In the South the war is what A.D. is elsewhere; they date from it.

MARK TWAIN

North, South, East, and West

Among the more elderly inhabitants of the South I found a melancholy tendency to date every event of importance by the late war. "How beautiful the moon is tonight," I once remarked to a gentleman who was standing next to me. "Yes," was his reply, "but you should have seen it before the war."

OSCAR WILDE

Everybody looks on this Civil War Centennial in a different light. Up in Harlem, all it means is the 100th anniversary of separate rest rooms. . . . That's why the South never suffered from Recession. Too busy building washrooms.

DICK GREGORY

Storytelling and copulation are the two chief forms of amusement in the South. They're inexpensive and easy to procure.

ROBERT PENN WARREN

Dust-stained, smelling of hot rubber and sheep-dip, with alfalfa seeds in my hair and my convertible ankle-deep in peanut-shells, I reached the Middle West after driving for about three weeks in a dead straight line along a highway, stopping only for gas, water, hot-dogs, gophers, highway patrols, road-blocks, landslides, stick-ups, floods, free air and unfenced cattle.

ALEX ATKINSON

29

"BUT I WOULDN'T WANT TO LIVE THERE!"

One thing I'll say fer the West is that in this country there is more cows and less butter, more rivers and less water, and you can look farther and see less than in any other place in the world.

SOUTHWESTERN RANCHER, QUOTED BY STAN HOIG

Yellowstone Park is no more representative of America than is Disneyland.

JOHN STEINBECK

I am bound to say at the outset that the Middle West was something of a disappointment to me, because it turned out to be in the north.

ALEX ATKINSON

If honesty were a national license plate policy, we'd see:

- RHODE ISLAND—LAND OF OBSCURITY
- OKLAHOMA—THE RECRUITING VIOLATIONS STATE
- MINNESOTA—TOO DAMN COLD
- WISCONSIN—EAT CHEESE OR DIE
- CALIFORNIA—FREEWAY CONGESTION WITH OCCASIONAL GUNFIRE
- NEW JERSEY—ARMPIT OF THE NATION
- NORTH DAKOTA—INCREDIBLY BORING
- NEBRASKA—MORE INTERESTING THAN NORTH DAKOTA
- NEW YORK—WE'RE NOT ARROGANT, WE'RE JUST BETTER THAN YOU

MOLLY IVINS

The Bicoastal Zone

CALIFORNIA

California is a great place to live if you're an orange.

FRED ALLEN

Californians are a race of people; they are not merely inhabitants of a State.

O. HENRY

Californians invented the concept of life-style. This alone warrants their doom.

DON DELILLO

Whatever starts in California unfortunately has an inclination to spread.

JIMMY CARTER

31

In California, everyone goes to a therapist, is a therapist, or is a therapist going to a therapist.

TRUMAN CAPOTE

California is a tragic country—like Palestine, like every Promised Land.

CHRISTOPHER ISHERWOOD

In California, every stretch of road—I don't care whether it's interstate or a state highway or a country road or gravel or asphalt or oil—all of it is nihilistic.

IAN FRAZIER

The west coast of Iowa.

JOAN DIDION

All creative people should be required to leave California for three months every year.

GLORIA SWANSON

The Bicoastal Zone

Living in California adds ten years to a man's life. And those extra years I'd like to spend in New York.

HARRY RUBY

A wet dream in the mind of New York.

ERICA JONG

. . .The worst thing you can say to a Californian is to tell him how much you like Florida.

C. V. R. THOMPSON

California is the only state in the union where you can fall asleep under a rose bush in the full bloom and freeze to death.

W. C. FIELDS

California, the department store state.

RAYMOND CHANDLER

"BUT I WOULDN'T WANT TO LIVE THERE!"

The Screwy State

ROBERT GRAVES

It's a shame to take this country away from the rattlesnakes.

ATTRIBUTED TO D. W. GRIFFITH

It's a scientific fact that if you stay in California, you lose one point of IQ for every year.

TRUMAN CAPOTE

California is a great spot for meeting people who come from some place else.

CHRISTOPHER ISHERWOOD

Oct. 23—Mild, balmy earthquakes.

Oct. 24—Shaky.

Oct. 24—Occasional shakes, followed by light showers of bricks and plastering . . .

Nov. 3—Make your will.

Nov. 4—Sell out . . .

Nov. 6—Prepare to shed this mortal coil.

Nov. 7—Shed.

MARK TWAIN

The Bicoastal Zone

All that is constant about California is the rate at which it disappears.

JOAN DIDION

Los Angeles

I mean, who would want to live in a place where the only cultural advantage is that you can turn right on a red light?

WOODY ALLEN AND MARSHALL BRICKMAN

There are two million interesting people in New York and only seventy-eight in Los Angeles.

NEIL SIMON

Fall is my favorite season in Los Angeles, watching the birds change colors and fall from the trees.

DAVID LETTERMAN

The difference between Los Angeles and yogurt is that yogurt has real culture.

TOM TAUSSIK

"BUT I WOULDN'T WANT TO LIVE THERE!"

The town is like an advertisement for itself; none of its charms are left to the visitor's imagination.

CHRISTOPHER ISHERWOOD

A big hard-boiled city with no more personality than a paper cup.

RAYMOND CHANDLER

There is always something so delightfully real about what is phony here. And something so phony about what is real. A sort of disreputable senility.

NOEL COWARD

Nineteen suburbs in search of a metropolis.

H. L. MENCKEN

Seventy-two suburbs in search of a city.

ATTRIBUTED TO DOROTHY PARKER

Nothing is wrong with Southern California that a rise in the ocean level wouldn't cure.

ROSS MCDONALD

Southern California, where the American Dream came too true.

LAWRENCE FERLINGHETTI

In Southern California the vegetables have no flavor and the flowers have no smell.

H. L. MENCKEN

L.A. is the loneliest and most brutal of America's cities; New York gets god-awful cold in the winter but there's a feeling of wacky comradeship in some streets. L.A. is a jungle.

JACK KEROUAC

Perhaps there is no life after death . . . there's just Los Angeles.

RICH ANDERSON

"BUT I WOULDN'T WANT TO LIVE THERE!"

Pick your enemies carefully or you'll never make it in Los Angeles.

RONA BARRETT

Ask a Kansas City man what is wrong with his town and he will probably attack you; and as for Los Angeles—! Such a question in Los Angeles would mean calling out the National Guard, the Chamber of Commerce, the Rotary Club, and all the "boosters" (which is to say the entire population of the city); the declaring of martial law, a trial by summary court martial, and your immediate execution.

JULIAN STREET

Hollywood is like Picasso's bathroom.

CANDICE BERGEN

Hollywood—an emotional Detroit.

LILLIAN GISH

Living in Hollywood is like living in a lit cigar butt.

PHYLLIS DILLER

The Bicoastal Zone

A dreary industrial town controlled by hoodlums of enormous wealth.

S. J. PERELMAN

Hollywood's a place where they'll pay you a thousand dollars for a kiss, and fifty cents for your soul.

MARILYN MONROE

Hollywood is a sewer—with service from the Ritz-Carlton.

WILSON MIZNER

Hollywood is where, if you don't have happiness, you send out for it.

REX REED

Hollywood money isn't money. It's congealed snow, melts in your hand, and there you are.

DOROTHY PARKER

They don't throw their garbage away. They make it into television shows.

WOODY ALLEN AND MARSHALL BRICKMAN

"BUT I WOULDN'T WANT TO LIVE THERE!"

Hollywood is a place where people from Iowa mistake each other for movie stars.

FRED ALLEN

A place where they shoot too many pictures and not enough actors.

WALTER WINCHELL

I'm not a little girl from a little town making good in a big town. I'm a big girl from a big town making good in a little town.

MAE WEST

If you stay in Beverly Hills too long you become a Mercedes.

ROBERT REDFORD

If you live in Beverly Hills they don't put blinkers in your car. They figure if you're that rich you don't have to tell people where you're going.

BETTE MIDLER

The Bicoastal Zone

I have a theory about L.A. architecture. I think all the houses had a costume party and they all came as other countries.

MICHAEL O'DONOGHUE

There are two modes of transport in Los Angeles: car and ambulance. Visitors who wish to remain inconspicuous are advised to choose the latter.

FRAN LEBOWITZ

Things to do in Burbank:
1. Go to the Safeway parking lot for the roller skating festival called Holiday on Tar.

JOHNNY CARSON

. . .The first American experimental space colony on earth.

HERBERT GOLD

[Malibu]: I had not before 1971 and will probably not again live in a place with a Chevrolet named after it.

JOAN DIDION

San Francisco and Beyond

We get baseball weather in football season and football weather in July and August.

HERB CAEN

The coldest winter I ever spent was a summer in San Francisco.

MARK TWAIN

When you get tired of walking around San Francisco, you can always lean against it.

TRANSWORLD GETAWAY GUIDE, 1975–1976

In San Francisco, Halloween is redundant.

WILL DURST

The Bicoastal Zone

San Francisco is like granola: Take away the fruits and nuts and all you have are the flakes.

UNKNOWN

Nothing important has ever come out of San Francisco, Rice-A-Roni aside.

MICHAEL O'DONOGHUE

Isn't it nice that people who prefer Los Angeles to San Francisco live there?

HERB CAEN

What was the use of my having come from Oakland it was not natural to have come from there yes write about it if I like or anything if I like but not there, there is no there there.

GERTRUDE STEIN

The trouble with Oakland is that when you get there, it's there.

HERB CAEN

NEW YORK, NEW YORK

The trouble with New York is it's so convenient to everything I can't afford.

JACK BARRY

An interesting thing about New York City is that the subways run through the sewers.

GARRISON KEILLOR

It's a town you come to for a short time.

ERNEST HEMINGWAY

New York is an exciting town where something is happening all the time, most of it unsolved.

JOHNNY CARSON

The Bicoastal Zone

New York now leads the world's great cities in the number of people around whom you shouldn't make a sudden move.

DAVID LETTERMAN

What else can you expect from a town that's shut off from the world by the ocean on one side and New Jersey on the other?

O. HENRY

New York is the only city in the world where you can get deliberately run down on the sidewalk by a pedestrian.

RUSSELL BAKER

There's no room for amateurs, even in crossing the street.

GEORGE SEGAL

"BUT I WOULDN'T WANT TO LIVE THERE!"

New York attracts the most talented people in the world in the arts and professions. It also attracts them in other fields. Even the bums are talented.

EDMUND LOVE

The Sheridan Apartment House stands in the heart of New York's Bohemian and artistic quarter. If you threw a brick from any of its windows, you would be certain to brain some rising interior decorator, some Vorticist sculptor or a writer of revolutionary *vers libre*.

P. G. WODEHOUSE

Friends come to visit New Yorkers a lot, because New York is a nice place to visit, but the hotel-room prices are prohibitive.

WILLIAM GEIST

New York is, after all, a place of business; it is not constructed to be lived in.

WYNDHAM LEWIS

Skyscraper National Park

KURT VONNEGUT

Prison towers and modern posters for soap and whiskey.

FRANK LLOYD WRIGHT

New York: the only city where people make radio requests like "This is for Tina—I'm sorry I stabbed you."

CAROL LEIFER

New York is getting like Paris. Its supposed devilment is its biggest ad. The rest of the country drop in here and think that if they don't stay up till four A.M. that New Yorkers will think they are yokels, when, as a matter of fact, New Yorkers have been in bed so long, they don't know what the other half is doing. New York lives off the out-of-towner trying to make New York think he is quite a fellow.

WILL ROGERS

"BUT I WOULDN'T WANT TO LIVE THERE!"

I suspect New York is as different from mainland America as Botswana. For the longest time after moving here from the Midwest, I thought everybody in New York was just running a fever—some sort of tsetse fly deal.

WILLIAM GEIST

I miss the animal buoyancy of New York, the animal vitality. I did not mind that it had no meaning and no depth.

ANAÏS NIN

When an American stays away from New York too long something happens to him. Perhaps he becomes a little provincial, a little dead and afraid.

SHERWOOD ANDERSON

It's a city where everyone mutinies but
no one deserts.

HARRY HERSHFIELD

This is New York, a combat zone, and everyone has to have an angle or they're not allowed over the bridges or through the tunnels.

CYNTHIA HEIMEL

The Bicoastal Zone

The city of right angles and tough, damaged people.

PETE HAMILL

New York is a sucked orange.

RALPH WALDO EMERSON

New York, the nation's thyroid gland.

CHRISTOPHER MORLEY

There are 36,000 vagrants in New York City and in two days of walking around every one of them asked me for money. Some of them asked twice.

People in New York go to Calcutta to get some relief from begging.

BILL BRYSON

. . . I've been a New Yorker for ten years, and the only people who are nice to us turn out to be Moonies.

P. J. O'ROURKE

"BUT I WOULDN'T WANT TO LIVE THERE!"

> **Rudeness is the privacy of New Yorkers.**
>
> THOMAS GRIFFITH

Personally, I've always favored New York 'cause this is one city where you don't have to ride in the back of the bus. Not that they're so liberal—it's just that in New York, nobody moves to the back of the bus!

DICK GREGORY

If there ever was an aviary overstocked with jays it is that Yaptown-on-the-Hudson called New York.

O. HENRY

What makes New York so dreadful, I believe, is mainly the fact that the vast majority of its people have been forced to rid themselves of one of the oldest and most powerful of human instincts—the instinct to make a permanent home.

H. L. MENCKEN

50

Greenwich Village is the Coney Island
of the soul.

MAXWELL BODENHEIM

[Wall Street]: A thoroughfare that begins in a graveyard and ends in a river.

ANONYMOUS

It's not Mecca, it just smells like it.

NEIL SIMON

Proposed name for the subway in the
Bronx: "The Bronchial Tube."

DR. L. BINDER

The Bronx?
No thonx.

OGDEN NASH

"BUT I WOULDN'T WANT TO LIVE THERE!"

If you live in New York, even if you're Catholic, you're Jewish.

LENNY BRUCE

Someone did a study of the three most-often-heard phrases in New York City. One is "Hey taxi." Two is "What train do I take to get to Bloomingdales?" And three is "Don't worry, it's only a flesh wound."

DAVID LETTERMAN

The most irritating thing of all is that New Yorkers really don't care what you say about their city.

RUSSELL BAKER

The Great In-Between

ALABAMA

Alabama . . . seems to have a bad name even among those who reside in it.

J. S. BUCKINGHAM

Birmingham is not like the rest of the state. It is an industrial monster sprung up in the midst of a slow-moving pastoral.

CARL CARMER

The only thing I didn't like about Birmingham was that when you blew your nose in the morning you wondered if you hadn't been cleaning chimneys in your sleep.

ERNIE PYLE

Mobile is a deceptive word. It sounds quick and yet it suggests immobility—glassiness.

HENRY MILLER

ALASKA

A handful of people clinging to a sub-continent.

JOHN MCPHEE

The Official State Motto of Alaska is: "Brrrr!" The Official State Bird is covered with oil.

DAVE BARRY

Compared to Fairbanks, Anchorage seemed like San Francisco.

JOE MCGINNISS

Seward's icebox.

NICKNAME USED AFTER SECRETARY OF STATE WILLIAM H. SEWARD SIGNED A TREATY FOR THE PURCHASE OF ALASKA FROM RUSSIA

. . . in Alaska. . . . You dare not perspire; your clothes would freeze on you. To get your feet wet is to lose your feet. To touch a piece of metal is worse than a bad burn.

ERNIE PYLE

. . . In the making of the world God grew tired, and when He came to the last barrowload, "just dumped it anyhow," and that was how Alaska came to be.

JACK LONDON

ARIZONA

Come to Arizona where the summer spends the winter.

(Slogan of state boosters)

And Hell spends the summer.

Addendum of local cynics.

H. L. MENCKEN

Arizona looks like a battle on Mars.

HARRISON SALISBURY

ARKANSAS

Happy is the state that has no history—and Arkansas has none. It was not founded by a pious Aeneas, nor fought over by Hannibals and Scipios. It just grew up out of seepage.

C. L. EDSON

I didn't make Arkansas the butt of ridicule. God did.

H. L. MENCKEN

It's irrelevant.

ROSS PEROT

COLORADO

There's no snob like an I'm-from-Colorado snob, unless it's an I'm-from-Colorado snob who was actually born in Colorado.

SAM MADDOX

This state has more sunshine and more bastards than any place on earth!

NANCY WOOD

Denver was not premeditated—it just happened.

ALICE POLK

CONNECTICUT

Little Connecticut . . . is made up, in almost equal parts, of golf links and squalid factory towns.

H. L. MENCKEN

Liberals have always been eunuchs in the court in Connecticut.

BILL MOYERS

DELAWARE

A state that has three counties when the tide is out, and two when it is in.

JOHN JAMES INGALLS

This is a small and measly state, owned by a single family, the Du Ponts. They made their money quarreling among themselves. Most of Delaware is but two or three feet above sea-level. It has no large city, and no person of any consequence has lived in it for half a century.

H. L. MENCKEN

FLORIDA

Florida was the only wilderness in the world that attracted middle-aged pioneers.

JOHN MCPHEE

It's a challenge for most Americans to visit Miami because it's bilingual. I still don't know what the other language is besides Spanish.

DAVE BARRY

Miami has now become the capital of Latin America.

JAIME ROLDOS

> **Miami Beach is where neon goes to die.**
>
> LENNY BRUCE

GEORGIA

I beg to present you as a Christmas gift, the city of Savannah with 150 guns and plenty of ammunition; and also about 25,000 bales of cotton.

GENERAL WILLIAM SHERMAN, IN A DISPATCH TO PRESIDENT LINCOLN

I have heard it said that the "architecture" of Atlanta is rococola. The pun is bad, but what the city would be like without Coca-Cola is hard to conceive.

JOHN GUNTHER

HAWAII

It is not surprising that Hawaii is so popular. At a time when theme parks are all the rage, Hawaii is the biggest theme park in the world.

FRANK DEFORD

59

Honolulu—it's got everything. Sand for the children, sun for the wife, sharks for the wife's mother.

KEN DODD

ILLINOIS

Hell had been described as a pocket edition of Chicago.

ASHLEY MONTAGU

Here is the difference between Dante, Milton and me. They wrote about hell and never saw the place. I wrote about Chicago after looking the place over for years and years.

CARL SANDBURG

No city ever owed its poets more. No poets could owe any city less.

NELSON ALGREN

The Great In-Between

You can say this about Chicago—there's no hypocrisy problem there. There's no need for hypocrisy. Everyone's proud of being a bastard.

SAUL BELLOW

Chicago is not the most corrupt American city—it's the most theatrically corrupt.

STUDS TERKEL

Chicago is as full of crooks as a saw
with teeth.

JOHN GUNTHER

Chicago—a facade of skyscrapers facing a lake and behind the facade every type of dubiousness.

E. M. FORSTER

Chicago is an October sort of city even in spring.

NELSON ALGREN, AS QUOTED BY GEORGE F. WILL

IOWA

Des Moines is the most powerful hypnotic known to man. Outside town there is a big sign that says, WELCOME TO DES MOINES. THIS IS WHAT DEATH IS LIKE.

When I was growing up I used to think that the best thing about coming from Des Moines was that it meant you didn't come from anywhere else in Iowa. By Iowa standards, Des Moines is a mecca of cosmopolitanism, a dynamic hub of wealth and education, where people wear three-piece suits and dark socks, often simultaneously.

BILL BRYSON

Three millions yearly for manure
but not one cent for literature...

ELLIS PARKER BUTLER

KANSAS

Historians have now definitely established that Juan Cabrillo, discoverer of California, was not looking for Kansas, thus setting a precedent that continues to this day.

WAYNE SHANNON

When I was small, billboards thirty feet wide and fifteen feet high stood in fields along every roadside. In places like Iowa and Kansas they were about the only stimulation you got.

BILL BRYSON

LOUISIANA

This state's full of sapsucker, hillbilly, and Cajun relatives of mine, and there ain't enough dignity in the bunch of 'em to keep a chigger still long enough to brush his hair.

HUEY LONG, AS QUOTED BY MARSHALL FRADY

"BUT I WOULDN'T WANT TO LIVE THERE!"

They say Louisiana is somewhat like a banana republic, say Guatemala. That's not true. They speak better English in Guatemala.

JACK KNEECE

To this day, whenever I think of New Orleans, I also think of Sodom and Gomorrah.

JAMES BALDWIN

There is no architecture in New Orleans, except in the cemeteries.

MARK TWAIN

[New Orleans] is a town where an architect, a gourmet or a roue is in hog heaven.

GEORGE SESSIONS PERRY

MAINE

There are only two things that ever make the front page in Maine. One is a forest fire and the other is when a New Yorker shoots a moose instead of the game warden.

GROUCHO MARX

The Great In-Between

You can certainly learn to spell "moccasin" while driving into Maine, and there is often little else to do, except steer and avoid death.

E. B. WHITE

MARYLAND

I firmly believe that Maryland is the most improbable state in the Union.

GERALD W. JOHNSON

Baltimore: mile after mile of identical houses, all inhabited by persons who regard Douglas Fairbanks as a greater man than Beethoven. (What zoologist, without a blood count and a lumbar puncture, could distinguish one Baltimorean from another?)

H. L. MENCKEN

Baltimore's such a lousy town, Francis Scott Key went out in a boat to write "The Star Spangled Banner."

BILLY MARTIN

For more than a century Baltimore was known throughout the nation under the unsavory name of "Mobtown." The title owed its origin to the speed and frequency with which the citizenry found excuse to riot.

FRANCES F. BEIRNE

MASSACHUSETTS

I have just returned from Boston. It is the only thing to do if you find yourself there.

FRED ALLEN

Boston: a potter's field, a dissecting room. Mental decay in all its forms, but one symptom there is in common: the uneasy fear of ideas, the hot yearning to be correct at all costs, the thirst to be well esteemed by cads.

H. L. MENCKEN

Boston runs to brains as well as to beans and brown bread. But she is cursed with an army of cranks whom nothing short of a straitjacket or a swamp elm club will ever control.

WILLIAM COWPER BRANN

The cold in Boston is terrible. Everything is frozen, even the thoughts of the people are frozen.

KAHLIL GIBRAN

One feels in Boston, as one feels in no other part of the States, that the intellectual movement has ceased.

H. G. WELLS

MICHIGAN

Detroit is a simple homogenous organism which has expanded to huge size.

EDMUND WILSON

Detroit is Cleveland without the glitter.

UNKNOWN

MINNESOTA

Nearly 50 percent of Minnesota conversations are conducted through the side window of a car or pickup or while leaning on the fender or hood, 30 percent are conducted over a little lunch at the kitchen table, 15 percent in a rowboat, and the remaining 5 percent take place in movie theaters during the movie. According to a recent study.

HOWARD MOHR

St. Paul in 1855 . . . The rude town was like a great fish just hauled out of the Mississippi and still leaping and squirming on the ground.

F. SCOTT FITZGERALD

Where I come from, when a Catholic marries a Lutheran it is considered the first step on the road to Minneapolis.

The difference between St. Paul and Minneapolis is the difference between pumpernickel and Wonder bread.

GARRISON KEILLOR

The Great In-Between

MISSISSIPPI

When you're in Mississippi, the rest of America doesn't seem real. And when you're in the rest of America, Mississippi doesn't seem real.

BOB PARRIS MOSES

[A] Boston writer says mud is a thing of the past. America has conquered mud. . . . Well, galoshes may not be necessary on Beacon Hill, but here in the Mississippi Delta, hip boots will not suffice. It is muddy. Lord it is muddy.

CHARLES KURALT

Mississippians are serenely confident that they have the most colorful history of any state. Never mind that almost all of it concerns one lost concern or another.

BERN KEATING

MISSOURI

Be from Missouri, of course; but for God's sake forget it occasionally.

ELBERT HUBBARD

"BUT I WOULDN'T WANT TO LIVE THERE!"

It isn't necessary to have relatives in Kansas City in order to be unhappy.

GROUCHO MARX

Kansas City has a certain complex about being the gizzard of America.

RICHARD RHODES

MONTANA

Montanans are free if not especially imaginative cussers.

A. B. GUTHRIE, JR.

Montana seems to me to be what a small boy would think Texas is like from hearing Texans.

JOHN STEINBECK

NEBRASKA

Nebraska is proof that Hell is full, and the dead walk the earth.

LIZ WINSTON

The Great In-Between

Nebraska must be the most unexciting of all the states. Compared with it, Iowa is paradise. Iowa is at least fertile and green and has a hill. Nebraska is like a 75,000-square-mile bare patch.

BILL BRYSON

When an Omaha man . . . speaks of steak, one expects him to pull from his pockets a series of treasured snapshots of steaks.

PHILIP HAMBURGER

NEVADA

The country looks like a singed cat.

MARK TWAIN

Nevada is a tale of two cities. Three of every four Nevadans live in or just outside Las Vegas or Reno.

NEIL MORGAN

"BUT I WOULDN'T WANT TO LIVE THERE!"

Las Vegas was never meant to be seen
by day.

PETER S. BEAGLE

It would be difficult to conceive of a more remote and cheerless state than Nevada.

BILL BRYSON

Las Vegas is the only town in the world whose skyline is made up neither of buildings, like New York, nor of trees, like Wilbraham, Massachusetts, but signs.

TOM WOLFE

NEW HAMPSHIRE

I live in New Hampshire so I can get a better view of Vermont.

MAXFIELD PARRISH

The Great In-Between

NEW JERSEY

A barrel, tapped at both ends, with all the live beer running into New York and Philadelphia.

BENJAMIN FRANKLIN

The curtain rises on a vast primitive wasteland, not unlike certain parts of New Jersey.

WOODY ALLEN

The CIA spent eight million dollars to destabilize Allende in Chile. If we could get them to spend that money in Newark, we'd be in great shape.

ART BUCHWALD

A state where political honesty is usually discussed during a prosecutor's summations.

JIMMY BRESLIN

The semi-colon of the Eastern
seaboard—that's modern New Jersey.

IRVIN S. COBB

NEW MEXICO

[The Painted Desert]: . . . Some hidden navel of the world where the rivers disappear and the hot magma pushes the granite up into pinkish veins, like
geodesic hemorrhoids.

HENRY MILLER

[Santa Fe] is composed of [newcomers who are] human vacuum cleaners. They
go around sucking up elements of all the different cultures that are jumbled
together here.

PHILIP HAMBURGER

NEW YORK

I was disappointed with Niagara—most people must be disappointed with Niagara. Every American bride is taken there, and the sight of the stupendous waterfall must be one of the earliest, if not the keenest, disappointments in American married life.

OSCAR WILDE

In Buffalo, suicide is redundant.

A CHORUS LINE

NORTH CAROLINA

North Carolina has less alien blood per square inch than any other State in the Union. That is one good reason why she has less writers, less painters, less sculptors, and above all, less musicians, than practically any other State of equal resource: certainly any other State of equal bombast.

CAROLINA MAGAZINE OF THE STATE UNIVERSITY,

QUOTED IN H. L. MENCKEN'S *AMERICANA*

"BUT I WOULDN'T WANT TO LIVE THERE!"

OHIO

. . . I couldn't say whether the improbable and highly relative assertion that Cleveland is better now than it used to be is wrong or right. What I can say is that the view up the Cuyahoga as I crossed it on the freeway was of a stew of smoking factories that didn't look too clean or handsome. And I can't say that the rest of the town looked such a knockout either.

BILL BRYSON

A gourmet restaurant in Cincinnati is one where you leave the tray on the table after you eat.

UNKNOWN

A hundred years ago Cincinnati was often called Porkopolis because so many hogs were butchered and processed there.

J. C. FURNAS

I suppose the high-water mark of my youth in Columbus, Ohio, was the night the bed fell on my father.

JAMES THURBER

OKLAHOMA

Never eat Chinese food in Oklahoma.

BRYAN MILLER

OREGON

Oregon is only an idea. It is in no scientific way a reality.

PHILIP WYLIE

The green damp England of Oregon.

ALISTAIR COOKE

PENNSYLVANIA

Pennsylvania, with its rocky gorges and woodland scenery, reminded me of Switzerland. The prairie reminded me of a piece of blotting-paper.

OSCAR WILDE

"BUT I WOULDN'T WANT TO LIVE THERE!"

> I went to Philadelphia one day. The place was closed.
>
> W. C. FIELDS

> The whole place is formal, precise, and unattractive, leaving no impression upon the mind of the traveller, but that of weary sameness and provoking rectangularity. . .
>
> CHARLES MACKAY

> Philadelphia: all the filth and corruption of a big city; all the pettiness and insularity of a small town.
>
> HOWARD OGDEN

> . . . Philadelphia, a metropolis sometimes known as the City of Brotherly Love but more accurately as the city of Bleak November Afternoons.
>
> S. J. PERELMAN

> Six months' residence here would justify suicide.
>
> HERBERT SPENCER

. . . Philadelphia is so comfortably behind the times that a postman was said to have been shot in the streets after being mistaken for a Confederate soldier.

SHANE LESLIE

No more egregious error can be committed by the visitor to Gettysburg than to assume that the Battle of Gettysburg (July 1–3, 1863) is over. In fact, there is reason to believe that hostilities are only just beginning. Skirmishes take place all over town . . . in one form or another, every hour of the day.

PHILIP HAMBURGER

RHODE ISLAND

Rhode Island was settled and is made up of people who found it unbearable to live anywhere else in New England.

WOODROW WILSON

Texas could wear Rhode Island as a watch fob.

PAT NEFF

SOUTH DAKOTA

You could shoot a cue ball from the southern boundary of the state all the way to Canada and halfway to the North Pole.

HOLGER CAHILL

The Badlands look as you might expect the moon to look, if it were hot, a parched picture of the earth in exploding wrath.

DOUGLAS REED

[The Badlands]: A part of hell with the fires burnt out.

GEORGE ARMSTRONG CUSTER

TENNESSEE

Take of London for 30 parts; malaria 10 parts; gas leaks 20 parts; dewdrops gathered in a brickyard at sunrise 25 parts; odor of honeysuckle 15 parts. Mix. The mixture will give you an approximate conception of Nashville drizzle.

O. HENRY

TEXAS

If I owned Texas and Hell, I would rent out Texas and live in Hell.

PHILIP SHERIDAN

[Texas is] the place where there are the most cows and the least milk and the most rivers and the least water in them, and where you can look the farthest and see the least.

H. L. MENCKEN

Calling a taxi in Texas is like calling a rabbi in Iraq.

FRAN LEBOWITZ

"BUT I WOULDN'T WANT TO LIVE THERE!"

. . . everything in Dallas looks as if it's been built in the last thirty minutes. Dallas can drop a glass office tower on a field of mesquite for you while you're stuck on a freeway. The city has always been known for its progress, not to overlook its bombast. If the Alamo had been in Dallas, it would be the Hyatt-Alamo today.

DAN JENKINS

The only thing that smells worse than an oil refinery is a feedlot. Texas has a lot of both.

MOLLY IVINS

Like most passionate nations Texas has its own private history based on, but not limited by, facts.

JOHN STEINBECK

A rich man can commit almost any sin in the state of Texas and get away with it, except for one—he's not allowed to go broke.

DAN JENKINS

UTAH

The fertility of the land has been outstripped by the fertility of the people.

FEDERAL WRITERS' PROJECT, *UTAH: A GUIDE TO THE STATE*

VERMONT

There is no cure for Vermont weather. It is consistent only in its inconsistency.

NOEL PERRIN

As Maine goes, so goes Vermont.

JAMES A. FARLEY

VIRGINIA

Shout at Virginia, shake it, slap its face, jump on it—Virginia will open one eye, smile vaguely, and go to sleep again.

WILL ROGERS

"BUT I WOULDN'T WANT TO LIVE THERE!"

. . . the story is told of a Virginia lady who became extremely irritated with the mass of tourists visiting her state; she was promptly reminded those tourists brought more than one hundred million dollars a year to the state of Virginia. "But why," she protested, "couldn't they just send the money?"

CLEVELAND AMORY

WASHINGTON, D.C.

Washington is a city of Southern efficiency and Northern charm.

JOHN F. KENNEDY

Too small to be a state but too large to be an asylum for the mentally deranged.

ANNE M. BURFORD

The United States also contains some history, most of which is located in special humidity-controlled rooms in Washington, D.C., heavily guarded by armed civil servants.

DAVE BARRY

84

The Great In-Between

The District of Columbia is a territory hounded on all sides by the United States of America.

IRVING D. TRESSLER

So I came to Washington, where I knew I would be farther away from America than I could be on some foreign shore; not that I do not respect this as a good part of America but in its general routine the heart of America is felt less here than at any place I have ever been.

HUEY LONG

There are a number of things wrong with Washington. One of them is that everyone has been too long away from home.

ATTRIBUTED TO DWIGHT D. EISENHOWER

The only thing wrong is that sometimes the District of Columbia is one giant ear.

RONALD REAGAN

Washington is the only place where sound travels faster than light.

C. V. R. THOMPSON

85

"BUT I WOULDN'T WANT TO LIVE THERE!"

There's nothing so permanent as a temporary job in Washington.

GEORGE ALLEN

People only leave by way of the box—ballot or coffin.

CLAIBORNE PELL

The only town in America where nouveaux is laudatory.

SALLY QUINN

It uses marble like cotton wool. It is the home of government of, for, and by the people, and of taste for the people—the big, the bland, and the banal.

ADA LOUISE HUXTABLE

Washington, D.C., Aug. 26 . . . Why, if they could get this Capitol moved away from here this would be one of the best towns in America.

WILL ROGERS

The Great In-Between

When I first went to Washington, I thought, what is l'il ole me doing with these ninety-nine great people? Now I ask myself, what am I doing with these ninety-nine jerks?

S. I. HAYAKAWA

Washington lies securely in what the guidebooks call an amphitheater and what you and I call a swamp.

ALISTAIR COOKE

I love to go to Washington—if only to be near my money.

BOB HOPE

WEST VIRGINIA

On the map my state is probably the funniest-looking state in the Union; it resembles a pork chop with the narrow end splayed.

JOHN KNOWLES

87

"BUT I WOULDN'T WANT TO LIVE THERE!"

WISCONSIN

In Green Bay, Wisconsin, ten bowling shirts are considered a great wardrobe.

GREG KOCH

WYOMING

Here is America high, naked, and exposed; this is a massive upland almost like Bolivia.

JOHN GUNTHER

Wyoming is a land of great open spaces with plenty of elbow room. . . .

FEDERAL WRITERS' PROJECT

It's all a bunch of nothing—wind and rattlesnakes—and so much of it you can't tell where you're going or where you've been and it don't make much difference.

RANCH HAND, AS QUOTED BY GRETEL EHRLICH

We the People

Americans like fat books and thin women.

RUSSELL BAKER

Americans have always been eager for travel, that being how they got to the New World in the first place.

OTTO FRIEDRICH

We are, after all, a country full of people who came to America to get away from foreigners.

P. J. O'ROURKE

All his life he (the American) jumps into the train after it has started and jumps out before it has stopped; and he never once gets left behind or breaks a leg.

GEORGE SANTAYANA

89

"BUT I WOULDN'T WANT TO LIVE THERE!"

We don't know what we want, but we are ready to bite somebody to get it.

WILL ROGERS

In America, unhappiness about the rat race is part of the people's happiness.

RALF DAHRENDORF

The American people, taking one with another, constitute the most timorous, sniveling, poltroonish, ignominious mob of serfs and goosesteppers ever gathered under one flag in Christendom since the end of the Middle Ages.

H. L. MENCKEN

America's dissidents are not committed to mental hospitals and sent into exile; they thrive and prosper and buy a house in Nantucket and take flyers in the commodities market.

TED MORGAN

Our system nurtures criminals with the same care the Air Force Academy uses to turn out second lieutenants.

JO WALLACH

90

We the People

Americans are getting like a Ford car—they all have the same parts, the same upholstering and make exactly the same noises.

WILL ROGERS

We take hamburgers more seriously than anyone else.

RAY KROC

Land of my dreams—Home of the Whopper.

BALKI BARTOKOMOUS, "PERFECT STRANGERS"

Well there is no danger in American culture of anything getting too clever or too pure or too refined in all its details.

HENRY MITCHELL

You can learn more about America by watching one half hour of "Let's Make a Deal" than you can get from watching Walter Cronkite for a month.

MONTY HALL

91

"BUT I WOULDN'T WANT TO LIVE THERE!"

Columbus has always seemed to me an odd choice of hero for a country that celebrates success as America does because he was such a dismal failure. Consider the facts: he made four long voyages to the Americas, but never once realized that he wasn't in Asia and never found anything worthwhile.

BILL BRYSON

After all, this is a nation that, except for a hard core of winos at the bottom and a hard crust of aristocrats at the top, has been going gloriously middle class for two decades.

TOM WOLFE

The great American tabernacle, the medicine cabinet.

PETER FASOLINO

Americans are remorseless. They invite you to a party. You can't say, "I've got a splitting headache"—they'll send the doctor around.

V. S. PRITCHETT

92

Don't tell me marriage is still a safe haven any place in America. Well, maybe among the Amish . . .

HERBERT GOLD

Americans are all too soft.

PEARL S. BUCK

It seems to be typical of life in America . . . that the second generation has no time to talk to the first.

JAMES BALDWIN

Americans drive across the country as if someone's chasing them.

CALVIN TRILLIN

We Are the World

I went around the world last year and you want to know something? It hates each other.

EDWARD J. MANNIX

I have recently been all round the world and have formed a poor opinion of it.

SIR THOMAS BEECHAM

It is a pity that people travel in foreign countries; it narrows their minds so much.

G. K. CHESTERTON

To travel is to discover that everyone is wrong about other countries.

ALDOUS HUXLEY

94

The great and recurring question about abroad is, is it worth getting there?

DAME ROSE MACAULEY

To feel at home, stay at home. A foreign country is not designed to make you comfortable. It's designed to make its own people comfortable.

CLIFTON FADIMAN

It is not a fragrant world.

RAYMOND CHANDLER

Travel is the most private of pleasures. There is no greater bore than the travel bore. We do not in the least want to hear what he has seen in Hong Kong.

VITA SACKVILLE-WEST

"BUT I WOULDN'T WANT TO LIVE THERE!"

The only people flying to Europe will be terrorists, so it will be, "Will you be sitting in armed or unarmed?"

ROBIN WILLIAMS

Never trust anything you read in a travel article. Travel articles appear in publications that sell large, expensive advertisements to tourism-related industries, and these industries do not wish to see articles with headlines like: URUGUAY: DON'T BOTHER.

DAVE BARRY

Those who go overseas find a change of climate, not a change of soul.

HORACE

The time to enjoy a European tour is about three weeks after you unpack.

GEORGE ADE

Africa

This Continent of Africa has a terribly strong sense of sarcasm.

DENYS FINCH HATTON,
QUOTED BY KAREN BLIXEN

. . . Life in Africa is nasty, British and short.

PAUL THEROUX

In Africa it is always five minutes to twelve.

ANONYMOUS,
QUOTED BY LORD HEMINGFORD

Never take a cold bath in Africa, unless ordered to do so by a doctor.

WILLIAM HENRY CROSS, M.D.

Nothing in Africa is adjacent to anywhere.

JAMES CAMERON

It is not the fully conscious mind which chooses West Africa in preference to Switzerland.

GRAHAM GREENE

EGYPT

I can't think much of a people who drew cats the same for four thousand years.

FIELD MARSHAL LORD KITCHENER

Could anything be wilder insanity than leaving a country like ours to see the bareness of mud?—Look! there is some water, and see! there is a crowd of people. They have collected with the purpose of drowning themselves.

RALPH WALDO EMERSON

Africa

Their strength is to sit still.

THE BIBLE, *ISAIAH 30:7*

[Cairo]: There is not perhaps upon earth a more dirty metropolis.

E. D. CLARKE

One cannot find the comforts of an English breakfast at Cairo.

JOHN CARNE

[The Pyramids] form the Hyde Park Corner of the Middle East.

LAWRENCE DURRELL

Asia

A kind of footnote to Persia.

JOHN GUNTHER

There is a proverb which says a visit to
Kunduz is tantamount to suicide.

ROBERT BYRON

CHINA

Very big, China.

NOEL COWARD

HONG KONG

To the naked eye, . . . Hong Kong's principal suburb was indistinguishable from
Asbury Park out of season.

S. J. PERELMAN

INDIA

"Sub-" is no idle prefix in its application to this continent.

P. J. O'ROURKE

The key of India is London.

BENJAMIN DISRAELI

Being Hindu means never having to say you're sorry.

GITA MEHTA

Indians love to reduce the prosaic to the mystic.

JAN MORRIS

It is a curious people. With them, all life seems to be sacred except human life.

MARK TWAIN

"BUT I WOULDN'T WANT TO LIVE THERE!"

Sikkim . . . is stuck between Bhutan and Nepal like a postage stamp.

VED MEHTA

The nightlife of Bombay is roughly on par with that of Schwenksville, Pennsylvania.

S. J. PERELMAN

India is a geographical term. It is no more a united nation than the Equator.

WINSTON CHURCHILL

JAPAN

The Japanese have perfected good manners and made them indistinguishable from rudeness.

PAUL THEROUX

102

Asia

The Japanese, whose game is what I may call make hell while the sun shines...

SIR WINSTON CHURCHILL

There are plenty of Japanese houses which, when secured for the night would hardly stand a drunken man leaning against them.

DOUGLAS SLADEN

It's so far away...and then you have to eat all that raw fish, drink tepid rice wine and live in cardboard houses.... And someone told me the toilet seats are much too small for my bottom...

W. H. AUDEN, QUOTED BY NICHOLAS NABOKOV

Japanese food is very pretty and undoubtedly a suitable cuisine in Japan, which is largely populated by people of below average size.

FRAN LEBOWITZ

[The Japanese] take snapshots of everything, not just everything famous but everything. Back in Tokyo there must be a billion color slides of street corners, turnpike off-ramps, pedestrian crosswalks, phone booths, fire hydrants, manhole covers and overhead electrical wires. What are the Japanese doing with these pictures? It's probably a question we should have asked before Pearl Harbor.

P. J. O'ROURKE

PAKISTAN

We eat dust, breathe dust and think dust.

T. E. LAWRENCE

RUSSIA

One Russian is an anarchist
Two Russians are a chess game
Three Russians are a revolution
Four Russians are the Budapest String Quartet

JASCHA HEIFETZ

Q: What is a Russian trio?

A: A Russian string quartet that has returned from the West.

DAVID STEEL

The Russians love Brooke Shields because her eyebrows remind them of Leonid Brezhnev.

ROBIN WILLIAMS

Russia is the only country of the world you can be homesick for while you're still in it.

JOHN UPDIKE

Russia—A riddle wrapped in a mystery inside an enigma.

WINSTON CHURCHILL

"BUT I WOULDN'T WANT TO LIVE THERE!"

Ideas in modern Russia are machine-cut blocks coming in solid colors; the nuance is outlawed, the interval walled up, the curve grossly stepped.

VLADIMIR NABOKOV

Moscow is the city where, if Marilyn Monroe should walk down the street with nothing on but shoes, people would stare at her feet first.

JOHN GUNTHER

[Moscow]...did look like the other side of the moon should look—gray, flat and spooky.

HARPO MARX

In Russia they treated me like a Czar—and you know how they treated the Czar.

BOB HOPE

Australia

Australia is not very exclusive. On the visa application they still ask if you've been convicted of a felony—although they are willing to give you a visa even if you haven't been.

P. J. O'ROURKE

Australian-based: a person of diminished aspiration who has been successfully bribed with grants and awards to resist the lure of expatriation.

Koala Triangle: a mysterious zone in the Southern Hemisphere where persons of talent disappear without a trace.

BARRY HUMPHRIES

107

"BUT I WOULDN'T WANT TO LIVE THERE!"

The national sport is breaking furniture and the average daily consumption of beer in Sydney is ten and three quarters Imperial gallons for children under the age of nine.

P. J. O'ROURKE

Australia!
Land of ravaged desert, shark-infested
ocean and thirst-lashed outback.

PETER TINNISWOOD

Canada

Canada is the vichyssoise of nations—it's cold, half French, and difficult to stir.

STUART KEATE

Canada is useful only to provide me with furs.

MADAME DE POMPADOUR

A few acres of snow.

VOLTAIRE

Canada is a country whose main exports are hockey players and cold fronts. Our main imports are baseball players and acid rain.

PIERRE TRUDEAU

109

"BUT I WOULDN'T WANT TO LIVE THERE!"

Canada is the only country in the world that knows how to live without an identity.

MARSHALL McLUHAN

Canada is a country so square that even the female impersonators are women.

RICHARD BENNER

For some reason, a glaze passes over people's faces when you say Canada.

SONDRA GOTLIEB

Canada's national bird is the grouse.

STUART KEATE

Canada has never been a melting pot;
more like a tossed salad.

ARNOLD EDINBOROUGH

Canada

Where else in the world could you find another case like ours—three thousand miles of forts, and not a single frontier?

STEPHEN LEACOCK

Ottawa—a sub-arctic lumber village converted by royal mandate into a political cockpit.

GOLDWIN SMITH

Ottawa is a city where nobody lives, though some of us may die there.

MICHAEL MACKLEM

If the national mental illness of the United States is megalomania, that of Canada is paranoid schizophrenia.

MARGARET ATWOOD

Europe

I do not find Northern Europe an ideal zone for human habitation. It is a fine place for industrial productivity, but its climate breeds puritans and the terrible dictates of the Protestant Work Ethic. The Romans were right to pull out when they did.

KENNETH TYNAN

Say what you want about "land of opportunity" and "purpled mountains majesty above the fruited plain," our forebears moved to the United States because they were sick to death of lukewarm beer—and lukewarm coffee and lukewarm bath water and lukewarm mystery cutlets with mucky-colored mushroom cheese junk on them.

P. J. O'ROURKE

112

Europe

I do not see the EEC as a great love affair. It is more like nine middle-aged couples with failing marriages meeting at a Brussels hotel for a group grope.

KENNETH TYNAN

European Community institutions have produced European beets, butter, cheese, wine, veal and even pigs. But they have not produced Europeans.

LOUISE WEISS

Studies show that Europeans hardly ever even *take* showers.

DAVE BARRY

It is only Europeans who travel out of sheer curiosity.

JEAN CHARDIN

In America everything goes and nothing matters. While in Europe nothing goes and everything matters.

PHILIP ROTH

113

"BUT I WOULDN'T WANT TO LIVE THERE!"

BELGIUM

Belgium is the most densely populated country in Europe...the sprout was developed by Brussels agronomists, this being the largest cabbage a housewife could possibly carry through the teeming streets.

ALAN COREN

Belgium is known affectionately to the French as "the gateway to Germany" and just as affectionately to the Germans as "the gateway to France."

TONY HENDRA

FRANCE

I would have loved it—without the French.

D. H. LAWRENCE

What I gained by being in France was learning to be better satisfied with my own country.

SAMUEL JOHNSON

114

Europe

France is the most civilized country in the world and doesn't care who knows it.

JOHN GUNTHER

If the French were really intelligent, they'd speak English.

WILFRID SHEED

I like Frenchmen very much, because even when they insult you they do it so nicely.

JOSEPHINE BAKER

Boy those French, they have a different word for everything.

STEVE MARTIN

The Almighty in His infinite wisdom has not seen fit to create Frenchmen in the image of Englishmen.

WINSTON CHURCHILL

Frenchmen are like gunpowder, each by itself smutty and contemptible, but mass them together and they are terrible indeed!

SAMUEL TAYLOR COLERIDGE

A relatively small and eternally quarrelsome country in Western Europe, fountainhead of rationalist political manias, militarily impotent, historically inglorious during the past century, democratically bankrupt, Communist-infiltrated from top to bottom.

WILLIAM F. BUCKLEY, JR.

In France, 'fraternity,' 'equality,' and 'indivisible unity' are names for assassination.

RALPH WALDO EMERSON

France has neither winter, summer, nor morals—apart from these drawbacks it is a fine country.

MARK TWAIN

In fine art, France is a nation of born pedants.

GEORGE BERNARD SHAW

They have certainly got the credit of understanding more of love, and making it better than any other nation upon earth; but for my own part I think them arrant bunglers, and in truth the worst set of marksmen that ever tried Cupid's patience. To think of making love by sentiments!

LAURENCE STERNE

Where did this sense of style thing get started? The French are a smallish, monkey-looking bunch and not dressed any better, on average, than the citizens of Baltimore.

P. J. O'ROURKE

They aren't much at fighting wars anymore. Despite their reputation for fashion, their women have spindly legs. Their music is sappy. But they do know how to whip up a plate of grub.

MIKE ROYKO

117

The French drink to get loosened up for an event, to celebrate an event, and even to recover from an event.

GENEVIÈVE GÉRIN

Maybe the French will get a manned craft into space, if they can get a rocket strong enough to lift a bottle of wine.

DAVID BRINKLEY

A bad liver is to a Frenchman what a nervous breakdown is to an American. Everyone has had one and everyone wants to talk about it.

ART BUCHWALD

Germans with good food.

FRAN LEBOWITZ

Never was there a country where the practice of governing too much had taken deeper root, and done more mischief.

THOMAS JEFFERSON

Everything is on such a clear financial basis in France. It is the simplest country to live in. No one makes things complicated by becoming your friend for any obscure reason. If you want people to like you, you have only to spend a little money.

ERNEST HEMINGWAY

An expensive minefield between Dover and the Spanish border.

ROGER BRAY

France is a geographical necessity.

SIR ANTHONY EDEN, QUOTED BY LORD MORAN

France has no friends, only interests.

ATTRIBUTED TO CHARLES DE GAULLE

There's something Vichy about the French.

IVOR NOVELLO, QUOTED BY EDWARD MARCH

119

[Paris]: A loud modern New York of a place.

RALPH WALDO EMERSON

It is the ugliest beastly town in the universe.

HORACE WALPOLE

Paris is a hostile brilliant alien city.

VIRGINIA WOOLF

Parasites are residents of Paris.

ART LINKLETTER

The veneer of Paris is the thinnest in the world.

HILAIRE BELLOC

120

Most of the houses in France are made of Plaster of Paris.

LOUIS UNTEMEYER

Paris is a filthy hole.

BENJAMIN ROBERT HAYDON

Paris is a nasty city.

D. H. LAWRENCE

Paris seems to be full of American girls who are hiding from their mothers.

JAMES THURBER

Nostalgia is the city's cheapest commodity and everyone foreign gets it for free.

TAKI

Paris is terribly derisive of all absurd pretensions but its own.

RALPH WALDO EMERSON

121

Paris today is a city asleep. And snor-
ing loudly.

NED ROREM

The Parisian travels but little, he knows no language but his own, reads no literature but his own, and consequently he is pretty narrow and pretty self-sufficient.
However, let us not be too sweeping; there are Frenchmen who know languages
not their own: these are the waiters.

MARK TWAIN

We went to Cannes. Its eccentric houses, villas, and toy palaces are nearly all
built for pleasure; one could place the Pyramids, the Taj Mahal and Grant's Tomb
into the center of it and they would scarcely be noticed.

LUDWIG BEMELMANS

Normandy has a bad reputation for rain and on that account is called the pot
de chambre of France.

R. H. BRUCE LOCKHART

We have given you Lafayette and French fried potatoes.

O. HENRY

France is the only country where the money falls apart and you can't tear the toilet paper.

BILLY WILDER

The French will always be partly tigers and partly monkeys.

VOLTAIRE

How can you be expected to govern a country that has 246 kinds of cheese?

CHARLES DE GAULLE

GERMANY

One German makes a philosopher, two a public meeting, three a war.

ROBERT D. MACDONALD

Whenever the literary German dives into a sentence, this is the last you are going to see of him till he emerges on the other side of the Atlantic with his verb in his mouth.

MARK TWAIN

. . . German—a language. . .which was developed solely to afford the speaker the opportunity to spit at strangers under the guise of polite conversation.

THE NATIONAL LAMPOON ENCYCLOPEDIA OF HUMOR

Everything that is ponderous, vicious and pompously clumsy, all long-winded and wearying kinds of style, are developed in great variety among Germans.

FRIEDRICK WILHELM NIETZSCHE

The German people are an orderly, vain, deeply sentimental and rather insensitive people. They seem to feel at their best when they are singing in chorus, saluting or obeying orders.

H. G. WELLS

The larger the German body, the smaller the German bathing suit and the louder the German voice issuing German demands and German orders to everybody who doesn't speak German. For this, and several other reasons, Germany is known as "the land where Israelis learned their manners."

P. J. O'ROURKE

The German mind has a talent for making no mistakes but the very greatest.

CLIFTON FADIMAN

One could almost believe that in this people there is a peculiar sense of life as a mathematical problem which is known to have no solution.

ISAK DINESEN

If my theory of relativity is proven successful, Germany will claim me as a German and France will declare that I am a citizen of the world. Should my theory prove untrue, France will say that I am a German, and Germany will declare that I am a Jew.

ALBERT EINSTEIN

One thing I will say for the Germans, they are always perfectly willing to give somebody else's land to somebody else.

WILL ROGERS

It is untrue that Germans are bad drivers. They hit everything they aim at.

JOEY ADAMS

The East Germans manage to combine a Teutonic capacity for bureaucracy with a Russian capacity for infinite delay.

GORONWY REES

The new Germany. . . is stunning. The place looks upholstered.

PATRICK O'DONOVAN

GREECE

Everything in Greece takes just twice as long as it would anywhere else. In this country they just do not use time at all.

EVELYN WAUGH

Europe

If it's beauty you want, go to Italy, go to the Cotswolds, go to a museum: don't come to Athens, where something else may happen.

KEVIN ANDREWS

To people with delicate ears a stay in Athens is torture.

ETHEL SMYTH

Those who tiptoe around the Acropolis today in their thousands hardly realise that they are looking at something like an empty barn.

LAWRENCE DURRELL

HOLLAND

Like the Germans, the Dutch fall into two quite distinct physical types: the small, corpulent, red-faced Edams, and the thinner, paler, larger Goudas.

Apart from cheese and tulips, the main product of the country is advocaat, a drink made from lawyers.

ALAN COREN

ITALY

One seldom finds in Italy a spot of ground more agreeable than ordinary, that is not covered with a convent.

JOSEPH ADDISON

In Italy they seem to have found out how hot their climate is, but not how cold; for there are scarce any chimneys, and most of the apartments painted in fresco; so that one has the additional horror of freezing with imaginary marble.

HORACE WALPOLE

They spell it Vinci and pronounce it Vinchy; foreigners always spell better than they pronounce.

MARK TWAIN

This country has made an art of being
vanquished.

ANONYMOUS

It is not impossible to govern Italians.
It is merely useless.

BENITO MUSSOLINI

There is no Italian word for privacy.

PETER NICHOLS

In Italy, the whole country is a theatre and the worst actors are on the stage.

GEORGE BERNARD SHAW

The median Italian . . . is a cowardly baritone who consumes **78.3** kilometres
of carbohydrates a month and drives about a car slightly smaller than he is, looking for a divorce.

ALAN COREN

129

"BUT I WOULDN'T WANT TO LIVE THERE!"

[The Leaning Tower of Pisa]: Like most things connected in their first associations with school-books and school-time, it was too small. I felt it keenly.

CHARLES DICKENS

Naples traffic isn't a condition. It's a war in progress.

ERMA BOMBECK

[Venice]: A city for beavers.

RALPH WALDO EMERSON

"Venice is Coney Island," the manager of the Piggly-Wiggly meat department said, "with pigeons."

IRENE KAMPEN

The bathing, on a calm day, must be the worst in Europe: water like hot saliva, cigar-ends floating into one's mouth, and shoals of jelly fish.

ROBERT BYRON

. . .The Biggest Tunnel of Love in the World.

RUBE GOLDBERG AND SAM BOAL

[Vatican City]: A Baroque State the size of Hyde Park.

PATRICK O'DONOVAN

She said that all the sights in Rome were called after London cinemas.

NANCY MITFORD

Rome, Italy, is an example of what happens when the buildings in a city last too long.

ANDY WARHOL

Rome has more Churches and less preaching in them than any City in the World. Everybody wants to see where Saint Peter was buried, but nobody wants to try to live like him.

WILL ROGERS

Rome is the only European capital which each year must spend millions of pounds restoring ruins, restoring them at least to their state of ruin of 100 years ago.

GEORGE ARMSTRONG

"BUT I WOULDN'T WANT TO LIVE THERE!"

The Italians have had two thousand years to fix up the Forum and just look at the place.

P. J. O'ROURKE

LUXEMBOURG

On a clear day, from the terrace. . .you can't see Luxembourg at all. This is because a tree is in the way.

ALAN COREN

POLAND

There are few virtues that the Poles do not possess—and there are few mistakes they have ever avoided.

WINSTON CHURCHILL

Poland is a vast and flat land where the winds blow very hard in any direction, and when this happens not only the hats fly away, the heads also.

MIECZYSLAW RAKOWSKI, QUOTED BY ORIANA FALLACI

Poland is now a totally independent nation, and it has managed to greatly improve its lifesyle thanks to the introduction of modern Western conveniences such as food.

DAVE BARRY

[Warsaw]: Famous for mines of salt and yokes of iron.

GEORGE GORDON, LORD BYRON

SWEDEN

Cross-country skiing's not a sport, it's how a . . . Swede goes to the 7-Eleven.

DAN JENKINS

SWITZERLAND

In Italy for thirty years under the Borgias they had warfare, terror, murder, bloodshed and they produced Michelangelo, Leonardo da Vinci and the Renaissance. In Switzerland they had brotherly love, five hundred years of democracy and peace and what did they produce? The cuckoo clock.

GRAHAM GREENE

"BUT I WOULDN'T WANT TO LIVE THERE!"

The Swiss are not a people so much as a neat, clean, quite solvent business.

WILLIAM FAULKNER

Every time I arrive in the country, I'm reminded of the old joke about God creating Switzerland. God asked the Swiss people what they wanted in the way of a country. They said they wanted huge Alps, deafening streams, and beautiful pastures where their riotous cows could ring their disco bells through the night. God provided all this in three days. The first Swiss innkeeper was so pleased, he asked if there was something he could do for God in return. God said yes, as a matter of fact. He was a little thirsty. He would like a glass of milk. "Fine," said the innkeeper. "That will be ten francs."

DAN JENKINS

Switzerland is a curt, selfish, swinish country of brutes, placed in the most romantic region of the world.

GEORGE GORDON, LORD BYRON

The only interesting thing that can happen in a Swiss bedroom is suffocation by feather mattress.

DALTON TRUMBO

Europe

Switzerland is simply a large, humpy, solid rock, with a thin skin of grass over it.

MARK TWAIN

. . . the train passed fruit farms and clean villages and Swiss cycling in kerchiefs, calendar scenes that you admire for a moment before feeling an urge to move on to a new month.

PAUL THEROUX

The only nation I've ever been tempted to feel really racist about are the Swiss— a whole country of phobic handwashers living in a giant Barclays Bank.

JONATHAN RABAN

YUGOSLAVIA

The food in Yugoslavia is fine if you like pork tartare.

ED BEGLEY, JR.

Israel

In Israel, in order to be a realist, you must believe in miracles.

DAVID BEN-GURION

One thing they always tell you in Israel: the one about its being not a melting pot, but a pressure cooker.

JAMES CAMERON

Whatever else Tel Aviv lacked, there was no shortage of cement block.

S. J. PERELMAN

Israel

The Middle East threat is to the oily places, not the holy places.

SHIMON PERES, QUOTED BY DONALD TRELFORD

This is the land that flowed with milk and honey. As a matter of fact it flows now chiefly with stones.

LILIAN LELAND

How it affects one to be cheated in Jerusalem.

HERMAN MELVILLE

New Zealand

Terrible Tragedy of the South Seas.
Three million people trapped alive!

TOM SCOTT

You are now landing in New Zealand.
Everybody is requested to put their
watches back ten years.

ANONYMOUS

I believe I have now acquired the two greatest requisites for bushmen in New
Zealand, viz., the capability of walking barefoot, and the proper method of cook-
ing and eating fern root.

THOMAS BRUNNER

138

New Zealand

A little piece of Victoriana in the Antipodes.

TONY SIMPSON

If an English butler and an English nanny sat down to design a country, they would come up with New Zealand.

ANONYMOUS

Compared to England it is like the week after a bloodless and smiling revolution.

J. B. PRIESTLY

United Kingdom

ENGLAND

When it's three o'clock in New York, it's
still 1938 in London.

BETTE MIDLER

In order to appreciate England one has
to have a certain contempt for logic.

LIN YUTANG

England is not governed by logic, but
by acts of Parliament.

UNKNOWN

Deploring change is the unchangeable habit of all Englishmen.

RAYMOND POSTGATE

United Kingdom

Englishmen know instinctively that what the world needs most is whatever is best for Britain.

OGDEN NASH

If it is good to have one foot in England it is still better, or at least as good, to have the other out of it.

HENRY JAMES

England is only a little island where one cannot go far out of one's way.

ERIC LINKLATER

I did a picture in England one winter and it was so cold that I almost got married.

SHELLEY WINTERS

The climate of England has been the world's most powerful colonizing impulse.

RUSSELL GREEN

"BUT I WOULDN'T WANT TO LIVE THERE!"

I'm leaving because the weather is too good. I hate London when it's not raining.

GROUCHO MARX

A place you go to get bronchitis.

FRAN LEBOWITZ

The English find ill-health not only interesting but respectable and often experience death in the effort to avoid a fuss.

PAMELA FRANKAU

The Englishman fox-trots as he fox-hunts, with all his being, through thickets, through ditches, over hedges, through chiffons, through waiters, over saxophones, to the victorious finish: and who goes home depends on how many the ambulance will accommodate.

NANCY BOYD

London is too full of fogs—and serious people. Whether the fogs produce the serious people or whether the serious people produce the fogs, I don't know, but the whole thing rather gets on my nerves.

OSCAR WILDE

The most dangerous thing in the world is to make a friend of an Englishman, because he'll come sleep in your closet rather than spend ten shillings on a hotel.

TRUMAN CAPOTE

If you eliminate smoking and gambling, you will be amazed to find that almost all an Englishman's pleasures can be, and mostly are, shared by his dog.

ATTRIBUTED TO GEORGE BERNARD SHAW

An Englishman, even if he is alone, forms an orderly queue of one.

GEORGE MIKES

"BUT I WOULDN'T WANT TO LIVE THERE!"

There is such a thing as too much
couth.

S. J. PERELMAN

The English have an extraordinary ability for flying into a great calm.

ALEXANDER WOOLLCOTT

England is the most class-ridden country under the sun. It is a land of snobbery and privilege, ruled largely by the old and silly.

GEORGE ORWELL

The English are the only nation to have discovered the means of limiting the powers of the man whose portrait appears on their coins.

S. R. N. CHAMFORT

The English instinctively admire any man who has no talent and is modest about it.

JAMES AGATE

144

I think it is owing to the good sense of the English that they have not painted better.

WILLIAM HOGARTH

The English may not like music but they absolutely love the noise it makes.

SIR THOMAS BEECHAM

The English think incompetence is the same thing as sincerity.

QUENTIN CRISP

Say Britain, could you ever boast,-
Three poets in an age at most?
Our chilling climate hardly bears
A sprig of bays in fifty years.

JONATHAN SWIFT

145

"BUT I WOULDN'T WANT TO LIVE THERE!"

England is a paradise for women, and a hell for horses: Italy a paradise for horses, hell for women, as the diverb goes.

ROBERT BURTON

Contrary to popular belief, English women do not wear tweed nightgowns.

HERMIONE GINGOLD

Continental people have a sex life, the English have hot water bottles.

GEORGE MIKES

I don't know what London's coming to—the higher the buildings the lower the morals.

NOEL COWARD

We know no spectacle so ridiculous as the British public in one of its periodic fits of morality.

LORD MACAULAY

146

An Englishman thinks he is moral when he is only uncomfortable.

GEORGE BERNARD SHAW

The last time Britain went into Europe with any degree of success was on 6 June 1944.

DAILY EXPRESS

I'm in favor of liberalized immigration because of the effect it would have on restaurants. I'd let just about everybody in except the English.

CALVIN TRILLIN

If you want to eat well in England, eat three breakfasts.

W. SOMERSET MAUGHAM

England has forty-two religions and only two sauces.

VOLTAIRE

"BUT I WOULDN'T WANT TO LIVE THERE!"

There are in England sixty different religions and only one gravy, melted butter.

MARQUIS CARACCIOLI

All of Stratford, in fact, suggests powdered history—add hot water and stir and you have a delicious nourishing Shakespeare.

MARGARET HALSEY

Even today, well brought-up English girls are taught by their mothers to boil all veggies for at least a month and a half, just in case one of the dinner guests turns up without his teeth.

CALVIN TRILLIN

. . . If the British can survive their meals, they can survive anything.

GEORGE BERNARD SHAW

What two ideas are more inseparable than Beer and Britannia?

REVEREND SYDNEY SMITH

The English are not an inventive people; they don't eat enough pie.

THOMAS A. EDISON

Those comfortably padded lunatic asylums, which are known, euphemistically, as the stately homes of England.

VIRGINIA WOOLF

Living in England, provincial England, must be like being married to a stupid but exquisitely beautiful wife.

MARGARET HALSEY

England is my wife—America, my mistress. It's very good sometimes to get away from one's wife.

SIR CEDRIC HARDWICKE

IRELAND

I am troubled, I'm dissatisfied. I'm Irish.

MARIANNE MOORE

I showed my appreciation of my native land in the usual Irish way by getting out of it as soon as I possibly could.

GEORGE BERNARD SHAW

The Irish are a fair people—they never speak well of one another.

SAMUEL JOHNSON

The Irish do not want anyone to wish them well; they want them to wish their enemies ill.

HAROLD NICOLSON

The English and Americans dislike only some Irish—the same Irish that the Irish themselves detest, Irish writers—the ones that think.

BRENDAN BEHAN

Every St. Patrick's Day every Irishman goes out to find another Irishman to make a speech to.

SHANE LESLIE

My one claim to originality among Irishmen is that I never made a speech.

GEORGE MOORE

When anyone asks me about the Irish character, I say—look at the trees. Maimed, stark and misshapen, but ferociously tenacious. The Irish have got gab but are too touchy to be humorous.

EDNA O'BRIEN

"BUT I WOULDN'T WANT TO LIVE THERE!"

Charming, soft-voiced, quarrelsome, priest-ridden, feckless, and happily devoid of the slightest integrity in our stodgy English sense of the word.

NOEL COWARD

Ireland has the honor of being the only country which never persecuted the Jews—because she never let them in.

JAMES JOYCE

Politics is the chloroform of the Irish people, or, rather, the hashish.

OLIVER ST. JOHN GOGARTY

In some parts of Ireland the sleep which knows no waking is followed by a wake which knows no sleeping.

MARY WILSON LITTLE

SCOTLAND

No McTavish
Was ever lavish.

OGDEN NASH

Oats—a grain which is generally given to horses, but in Scotland supports the people.

SAMUEL JOHNSON

But all Scotchmen are not religious . . . some are theologians.

GERALD BENDALL

Is anything worn beneath the kilt?
No, it's all in perfect working order!

SPIKE MILLIGAN

It requires a surgical operation to get a joke well into Scottish understanding.

SYDNEY SMITH

153

"BUT I WOULDN'T WANT TO LIVE THERE!"

It is never difficult to distinguish between a Scotsman with a grievance and a ray of sunshine.

P. G. WODEHOUSE

WALES

There are still parts of Wales where the only concession to gaiety is a striped shroud.

GWYN THOMAS

A Welshman is a man who prays on his knees on Sundays and preys on his neighbors all the rest of the week.

ANONYMOUS

The land of my fathers. And my fathers can have it.

DYLAN THOMAS

Index of Places

Index of Sources

158